ONION RIVER
Six Vermont Poets

ONION RIVER

Six
Vermont
Poets

DANIEL LUSK, EDITOR

Acknowledgments

Special thanks to Susan Lafayette, Heather Laszlo, Anne Linton, Vicky McCafferty and Cathy Wood, to the Shelburne Museum, and to Mike DeSanto and Renée Reiner for their enthusiastic support of this project and for the establishment of The Book Rack reading series which first brought this group of poets together in April 1996.

Poems in this volume first appeared in the following literary journals:
EMILY SKOLER: *Passages North* ("Llegamos Sin Nada En Las Manos," "Stay," and "I'm glad"); *Dreaming of Amelia* ("Traveling Song"); *Third Coast* ("What is Jupiter").
KENNETH SCHEXNAYDER: *American Poetry Review* ("Towards Distant Water"); *Cutbank* ("For the First Time"); *Nimrod* ("For the Long Road," "Like a Stone in the Evening Sky"); *Southern Poetry Review* ("The Gray Heron"); *Tar River Poetry* ("Not All Faces"); *Willow Springs* ("Blackberries," "Like This").
ANGELA PATTEN: *The Eleventh Muse* ("Fire Song").
NORA MITCHELL: all the poems by Nora Mitchell were published in her collection titled *Proofreading the Histories* (AliceJames, 1996).
DOUGLAS K. CURRIER: *The Cafe Review* ("Metaphysics of Wool").
SUE D. BURTON: *Sinister Wisdom* ("Millet"); *Sojourner* ("What's Possible").

Cover art: "6 A.M. in Vermont," wood engraving, Asa Cheffetz, property of the Shelburne Museum (permission granted)
Cover Design: Vicky McCafferty, Burlington, Vermont
Layout and Design: MacWorks, Winooski, Vermont

R.N.M., Inc. is a publishing enterprise of Michael DeSanto and Renée Reiner, proprietors of The Book Rack and Children's Pages in the Champlain Mill, Winooski, Vermont.

Library of Congress Cataloguing-in-Publication Data
Lusk, Daniel
Onion River: Six Vermont Poets
ISBN 0-9657144-0-3
Library of Congress Catalog Card Number 97-66698

ABOUT THE COVER ARTIST

Cover artist: Asa Cheffetz (1896-1965) was
born in Buffalo, New York, and lived most of
his life in New England. Schooled in drawing
and painting at the School of the Museum of
Fine Arts and the National Academy of Design
in New York, beginning in 1927 with woodcuts,
he taught himself the ancient art of wood
engraving which was to become his life's work.
The engraving shown on the cover, "6 A.M. in
Vermont," was selected for showing at the
World's Fair in Chicago and Fifty Best Prints
of the Year 1934, which was exhibited in muse-
ums and exhibitions around the country. It is
among the many prints by the artist in the collection of the Shelburne Museum, Shelburne,
Vermont.

D.L.

FOREWORD

The poems in this collection represent much of what is honest
and good about the character and volume of poetry being made
in Vermont nowadays. Collectively, they reflect some of the tradi-
tional stuff and manner of poetry, but also much that is highly
individual and personal. From the first line of the opening poem
by Emily Skoler: "Just as one bird, uprising, sings la de dah, suddenly the mountain unzips miles of trail," to the last, by Sue
Burton, "We love you! Don't die young!.," these poems look vari-
ously inward and outward, sometimes (as in Nora Mitchell's "The
Flat Earth") simultaneously. Some reach backwards to other coun-
tries (as do Angela Patten's poems about Ireland) and to other
cultures (as do poems by Vermont native Doug Currier, bearing
influences of Argentina). Others look ahead as well (as does "For
the Long Road" by Ken Schexnayder).

This is a spirited collection of poets, each with a unique vision and
personal artistry. Out of pain and ecstasy, regret and thoughtful-
ness and insight, these poets show us the old faces of human the-
ater. And, while these are neither the eldest nor the youth among
the wealth of literary artists in our state, I believe they represent
the finest of an emerging community of poets contributing to cul-
tural life in Vermont and to the literary life of the country.

I am confident that readers will discover much to enjoy in these
poems, much of our shared landscapes, much that will prompt
personal memory and reflection, much of that which each poet,
by intimate weddings of common doings and epiphanies, has
made permanent.

Daniel Lusk
January 1997
Colchester, Vermont

Springtime

Just as one bird, uprising, sings la de dah, suddenly
the mountain unzips miles of trail.
And the sky has no latch!

Don't say anything, pretty bird.
Don't say the wood pile.
Don't say the tiny weightless.
Don't say winter waits around the bend.

Don't smile insanely sky;
dawn still lounges on window sills in the village.
Maps are worth nothing, pink and green paper.

My enemy is this polite
and dangerous weather, this
mischievous, rationed happiness.

Don't anybody move 'til it's over.

I'm glad

my father wasn't wearing a PARTY NOW
WORK LATER t-shirt
stretched across his gut
one late August afternoon
when he might have walked through town
like the man I saw today
with his young wife
and daughter. Instead,
he was at the factory
overseeing the newly-landed
as they dropped empty paint tubes
onto the conveyer belt for filling,
and screaming above the noise, perhaps, to stop Rodriguez
from loading a tray marked "Aquamarine"
under a nozzle squeezing out yellow,
the color of over two-hundred raincoats
my grandfather sewed sleeves into,
backwards, his second day in America.
Some woman who also didn't speak English
showed him how to hold tight
the wachamacallit, so
they let him keep that job
and soon he added several children
to a two-room apartment
and began peddling housewares on Sundays
with the other Jewish man in town,
whose son was one day
pushed from a garage roof
just a few blocks

from where my father pushed his sister
under a silver turnstile
so he could keep the nickel
for an ice cream cone.
I'm glad my father was too busy making money
to take us shopping
on a summer afternoon. He might have
embarrassed me with his black socks and sandals.
He might have said "lazy" or "stupid"
as we strolled by the man wearing that t-shirt.
I might never have gotten so far
feeling this superior and ashamed.

Llegamos Sin Nada En Las Manos

Evening paws at the screen.
Git, someone shouts, and tosses a bone
beyond his yard as if to trick the dark, but
the smell of damp fur rises and neighbors' windows

become boxes of light I will carry
through the night. Was it only last week
Suzy Juarez broke my corazon when she buttoned
up her blouse and marched back to her husband?

She didn't have a husband. Still,
who could stand another moment of
those large white teeth clinking the whiskey glass,
another night of those dangerous

hands? Whoever said "Happiness tastes
like a calcified stick," was right.
Whoever says we'll one day know
what the stars really stand for

is a liar. The stars wish they were less eternal and more
like us, like Suzy and me, women
sauntering away from each other with Spanish
stuck to the roofs of our mouths.

Now what's left for me but to walk
the electric neighborhood, past gas stations, bars,
and women in doorways kissing shadows
until someone taps my shoulder,

and turning, I see myself. "Little Pepita," I say,
"sí, we arrive without nothing in our hands."
"Please," says each star,
"don't wear out my name."

Many of Us Never

The sun feels so good
this time of year, seeping
through cotton. Our hair is warm to the touch.
Hot dogs roast on the grill

while plastic protects soft, white rolls
from noisy flies. When the beach ball lands in the pool
someone who isn't drunk tries
to reach it, over near the deep end.

Now the wind, starting
as a woman's high-pitched laughter, sweeps
into the yard, and the ball drifts
further from the edge.

A man with long arms comes over to help.
These chairs are so comfortable;
these drinks so cold.
Many of us never volunteer.

Not our hostess who's set down her glass to push
a strand of hair behind her ear.
Not the man who's just uncrossed
his legs and leaned forward or the woman

listening, who shakes her head,
splashing him with the idea she has
nothing on under her dress.
The ball, right where we can see it,

lends color to the water.
Hot dogs sizzle and juice.
Teenagers, holding each others' waists,
take turns and strain toward the middle

of the bright aqua rectangle.
A few touch the ball,
but it only spins on its axis, and never
gets any nearer. Someone walks away

from the clean yard toward the woods
to look for a stick and never comes back.

When the Houselights Come Up

Isn't grief appealing, cornered
in a glossy photo? You wrote, *pretend
your life is a movie,* so now I'm waiting for the camera
to find me tapping each cigarette empty of ash,
wearing an expression meant to empty me

of everything I still don't understand, and posing
for the occasional woman who looks my way
with the look you wore, that squint even at night
as if the sun were in your eyes. Here at the edge
of the park, a skateboarder jumps

the littered curb each time the light changes, wishing
his wheels into place beneath him.
I still don't understand
why you were more comfortable being wounded
than loved, or whether it had anything to do

with the charming fact that leukemia was named
for the bloom of leukocytes, white cells flowering
in the slow-motion of nature films. They say
white blossoms are among the most fragrant
in any garden, which accounts for the number

of moths, their frantic beating of wings, a longing
they're unable to contain. They say a moth
will exude the scent of flowers it visits, some white
and silky as dresses that might have fallen
to the floor. If only we'd been smart enough

to step from them. We were wrong about a lot of things.
I saw your favorite dancer in the shopping center
with her kids. Whatever grace we noticed
in the dark bar as we tilted the cold mouths
of beer bottles, she was just another woman

whose weariness shows when the houselights come up.
Or maybe grace is the ability to commit
to whoever we're with. The dancer went with the leash
of her son's arm when he dragged her
toward the vending machines. She leaned

into the music, edging closer
to our seats. The person next to me, swiveling a pink
vinyl stool at the Dunkin Donuts,
is never you anymore. Every time you slanted
a new cigarette toward the flame

cupped in my hand, I saw you didn't know
you were pretty. I like to think I would've told you that
the day I came looking for you here, and a thin, shirtless boy,
nipple rings glinting, said so easily, *She's dead.*
Maybe not. We never even kissed.

Traveling Song

Sometimes the trees along the highway.
The trees grow into the darkness
and the darkness grows.
Sometimes taillights from cars ahead.

On long drives
it comes back to me,
how loving you was like
having the flu.
It impressed me,
but I wanted it to be over.
I kept waiting to turn back into myself.

Sometimes the sun burns out
in the corner of the rear-view mirror
and I think of you, how I was forever
looking at you
through something else—usually

my desire. Songs on the radio
turn into static beneath overpasses,
then back into songs
under open sky.
I miss you. It comes and goes like that.

Stay

The sky is a bright blue leash.
I'm tethered to a street sign
where many pedestrians

decorated with lipstick and shoes find me
cute and think of touching
my ears. I've seen this afternoon

somewhere before, trying to paint the houses
a relevant yellow. But
compared with the boy

who holds his mother's hand and stops
to karate kick every lamp post
adorned with the enemy's long

mean teeth, the afternoon is unreal.
More real though than these moments
will seem to him years from now

when he wonders at being given a body
made for guiding itself
into another. As gently as I would

carry a green felt hat
in my mouth
back to a woman

from whose hairstyle
the wind has just lifted it.

What Is Jupiter?

Today they are opening up my friend
to see whether it's a Szechuan Chicken peanut
blocking her intestinal flow,
or just another tumor
to be shrunk and plucked.
For twelve hours they've been waiting
for her to fart. And this is just how she says it
over the phone. And I know
it's not a peanut.

The trees are covered in ice, and the wind
rubbing the branches together
makes a music which I equate with the body's
little trumpet farts
because it leaves me speechless,
embarrassed,
wondering who's responsible.

But so what. Everyone writing a poem today
in the cold and brilliant northeast is anthropomorphizing
    these trees,
making of them a symbol of the body's beauty
and fragility. And after awhile the rustling,
clinking branches become so annoying
I know they are my punishment
for lying.

Because my friend died years ago.

And if she'd had any idea what was ahead of her
she might have been a little less honest herself
and rolled her lips together while the nurse was fussing
with tubing and drip bags,
rolled her lips, blown out,
and emitted that sputtering sound
we practiced while our teachers' backs were turned.

It's how we come to understand ourselves, impersonating
each human strangeness. "Mmmmm, oohh,"
we tried just a few years later,
pillows pressed against our chests
as afternoon dwindled
to a red dot on patterned wallpaper. "Yes,"
we murmured into the laundry-fresh scent. "Oh
yes, sweetheart."

Is beauty supposed to
balance all the loss?

Who but the living
would insist on a connection between sex and death?

They sliced her from breastbone to groin,
which is what my friend really never recovered from,
an uncanny resemblance
to some frogs spilled open
before us in eighth grade biology lab:

formaldehyde drenched, skin pinned back to reveal
each little organ precisely in place,
so perfectly dead.

By the time I got there she was stapled shut,
bathed in the light of
a game show where the questions
were shaped like answers, the answers
shaped like questions.

I remembered this a few hours ago,
shoveling ice from my back steps.
Occasionally, a form of grief comes
that is neither question nor answer;
the simple desire to see her again.

Did I really lie? Did she die years ago?
It feels like today.
It feels like tomorrow I will visit her
and rub her feet between a blue hospital blanket
until she falls asleep. I'll stay and watch her sleep.
It feels like I have the courage finally
when she asks, "Am I alone?" to answer
"Yes." Even though at any moment
the night nurse will enter,
any moment the game-show host will stump me
with his next words: this planet would float
if we could put it in a bath tub big enough.

Self Portrait While Pretending I'm Someone Else

I believe Picasso when he says art lies
to tell the truth. I wonder, as Jean Cocteau did,
whether stories might just be
alibis. My jury is still out on Keats's claim
that beauty is truth, and vice-versa, though I admit I feel
most like myself
after I've rolled on some peacock blue eyeliner.
Come on, beauty is beauty,
and I never want another haircut
like the one when I was twelve.
It's ugliness that wants the truth.
Did you know,

you can bounce $50,000 worth of bad checks
before the FBI starts a file on you? Mine
would say my hair is brown and naturally curly,
but the fact is I want to be investigated
by my husband's hands as if I were a stranger
whose motives, morning breath, and childbearing
potential were as yet unknown to him.
I want a lover who thinks
he has to think like me
in order to track me down.
And though this doesn't explain desire,
it might have something to do with why I fall
for intellectual men, why
once I lied.

I cry so easily. I devour books.
My childhood was nothing
to write home about; now my own children
try to kill themselves—
this one with Ninja kicks, that one smearing the red
juice of unidentified berries across her mouth
so the boys in our small town will notice.

When I believe what I'm seeing,
I believe what I'm feeling. Description
is attitude, I'll instruct,
when the time comes
to talk dirty. I think, in my own words,
that truth is wary, and we can consider only the slant
of it as Emily Dickinson did
alone in a second-floor room, the sun
angling across her inky thoughts.

My name is Emily too,
though I share none of her loneliness.

I can see that if you want something
done right, you have to do it yourself,
which is why as the adult child
of antique dealers, I'm asking you to listen carefully.
I only want to say this once:
I thought he would think more highly of me
if he thought I'd had some articles accepted by a journal.
Just my luck the journal was defunct,
the editor his best friend.

Can I believe Benedetto Croce when he says it would be a
   mistake
to define falsehood as a failure
to tell the truth? I'm no stranger
to failure, but the truth is,
I thought I was in love.
That's how it was
when I was young—
any intelligent face set me spinning,
and I didn't look this good in pink.

Like This

Bless the reckless intrusion
of flowers, the sudden break
in the fierce habits seasons form.
Stars light, like birds onto a fence,
and a boy takes up a guitar,
strums the moon into a face.
We hunger for a confirmation
of ourselves with each new acquaintance.
Listen: a man and a woman
lie at night beneath a tree,
their whispered secrets
pollen, a fresh rustling in the wind.
A blackbird starts, shatters twigs.
It settles. Like this we begin.

The Gray Heron

The pallor of landscape lures me.
In its gray hand
the fog cups rocks.
In the noise of the creek
a heron feeds. I wade into the mist,
feel the tow entice my ankles. I believe
this fog could grip my life,
sweep it past the gray heron
to what lies downstream.
In that moment it seems
I've stood here always,
shoes in hand,
braced against the flow,
that pulls me farther
from the comfort of what is familiar,
towards my fear of what is not.
Before me the heron
breaks into cloud,
and rain begins
to fall on quiet stone.

Like a Stone in the Evening Sky
for Richard Hugo

With the moon worn to a crescent
and the sweet air heavy with alyssum
we sat beneath the cottonwoods,
whiskey on the table between us.
Your speech was dull: no flash
of rainbow or cutthroat, nor of the possibilities
their arched bodies held for you
in sunlight. Life is generous, you said,
only for the man who uncurls himself
from the stone in his belly,
the core of his fidelities,
who stands apart in the crowded centers,
open to the rush of voices and longing of prayers.

Your long illness hung dark as that night over your life.
And you measured recovery like the approach of dawn,
a gradual graying towards brilliance.
But nothing played as vibrant in that new light.
Not sun on the lake's surface
nor on the bellies of trout.
Not your own work that gave you sustenance.
You asked that I imagine the moon a stone in the evening sky
and the sky our blood, sweat, tissue, our longing.
In that cosmology, life's more sadness than joy,
the essential touch of flesh absent.
But in this good life, sheltered by leaves,
two men fell that night into each other's arms
under the waning moon,
believing the light builds anew
each time it fails to black.

For the Long Road

Not the rich flame of a maple
that stops us this time,
but twenty-four Guernsey, in the chill
and drizzle, winding nose to tail
up the dirt road.

I snatch my camera,
stumble through clumps
of wet grass and mats of fallen leaves
to photograph what already changes.
Through the lens I see
the line of cattle broken,
the panic as they run
in twos and threes away from me.

I turn to my wife,
framed in the car's open window
and frame her again in the camera.
I see clearly the face I've grown to trust,
and in the chill and drizzle
the trust as what I believe will sustain me.
In that instant
I feel an old sorrow
rise from the bone, a regret
for what I have not said to her
and for the long road
down which my many silences have led us,
to arrive in this late season,
a shock of autumn maple above,

the wet earth below
growing colder
as it turns toward winter.

Not All Faces

That not all faces turn up
into the flowering heat
simply confirms diversity: the prospect
of any poplar containing within its silver,
blackbirds, the possibility of not.
Perhaps sound, scratching branches, or
perhaps the silence of winter.
With either that we find, we must be content.
A small boy with a pellet rifle
holds a dying bird. Asks forgiveness.
Around him continues
the relentless migration,
the reasoned patterns of flocks,
loose leaves in the air.

As We Lie Down to Sleep

Face bright from the October chill,
my daughter laughs and rolls
in the spotfires of maple and oak
I've raked into piles. She plays
as the trees rush towards dormancy,
and my own grief shakes loose
as I see again my father
who lay down to sleep
among autumn leaves,
whose sleep became my own
as I closed my eyes
to that season, then gradually woke,
holding that cold dark inside.

Today the trees cast harsh shadows
and leaves light the grass.
A season of resemblances:
my daughter a reflection of my youth,
me of my father and the dreams hung
on the bright future of his young son.
She runs to me and I lift her.
We fall into a mound of leaves.
Then she's gone from my arms
into the clear light of October
where she crashes again and again,
fair-skinned and precious,
into the fallen leaves.

For the First Time

Cockatoos gnaw the heart from papaya,
leaving yellow streaked skins.
On the reef at morning,
blue starfish abandoned by the tide.
Take these events as signifiers,
not for the grief of loss
we fear our children will know,
forests gone, the sea a carrier
of pestilence, but for design,
the way men or women lift their eyes
after a mistake, seize some inner knot of strength
and tie a stronger one.

The moment of clarity matters:
the slow warmth of satisfaction
when for the first time I saw
in humus fertility and not death.
As in the letter I wrote my friend,
trying to explain my leaving,
that the ocean between us
is not simply abrasive waves, a stripping away.
It has more to do with how the gravel reassembles
as each wave dies. The continual reorganization.
The sharp red as a lory darts from a coconut palm.
Daily I walk down to the stream to bathe,
sit with the water to my neck.
Fallen leaves appear
to move against the flow,
as the salt from the sea
moves upward from the mouth.

Blackberries

Alluring
in their dark

enclave
they hang full, ripe,

entice fingers
to enter briers.

Inside
a serpent coils,

strikes,
leaves its purple stain

of longing.
Its tongue appears

suddenly,
offers two paths to follow.

Towards Distant Water

1
The bluffs we drive from
sink slowly into what
must be the river, the gap
where Wolf River bites
into the Mississippi already gone.

We can close our eyes
to death. I close mine
to these Arkansas fields
and open them
to stark paddies, people
bent at the waist, their pants
bound tightly to their calves.

Some straighten and wave.
Others mouth greetings
I cannot hear.
They grow and blur
then sharpen into streaks
of rain on glass.
The road climbs

from farmlands to mountains,
from farmers to folks.
You're singing again, a song
from these hills, how on a Sunday
a family gathers around a grave,
shovels earth with their own hands.
They bury their dead only once.

2

At sunset, near El Paso,
we scrape bones from the ground
with our boots,
stake our tent to the desert
between two cacti and pour water
quickly over our hands, shivering.
In silence we sit at the fire,
hearing restless movement,
the shadows just beyond the bones.
You hold your fiddle
close at your neck. I watch the fire perform.
The song, from back home,
draws the darkness towards the flame.
Above, the Texas stars begin
their slow circle, pulling up,
growing more distinct as they turn.

3

At eight in the morning
we cross the border.
At a cafe table
with beans, tortillas, beer,
and half a dozen hostile stares,
I feel a voice
that has followed me for days,
haunted me from billboards,
called to me with wrinkled feet.
I begin to see

more than empty palms, ragged
shoots of rice, more than
a kid asking how much
I'll pay for a woman.

4
At the church door, a stooped woman
speaks to us of candles,
collects money for a funeral.
We don't know the man
padlocked in a glass casket,
but pretend to look at the architecture,
the tense symmetry of tile.
We steal an occasional glance

at lips moving in silent prayer,
fingertips touching holy water
as if it were hot, pressing
its warmth between eyes.
Even in church I fear the water,
sprinkled and running on glass.

The Garden

Miyazaki, Japan

The clap of hands
attracts carp, churning

hungry, white and gold.
Similarly the wandering

mind snaps back
as the zen master slaps

hard his *shinai*
across the beginner's shoulder.

In among the limbs
the *ueki-ya* clips

new growth
from the *bonsai*.

I walk the path,
my mind too playfully

western this morning
for meditation.

I recall Tsugiko,
a young poet,

and the night
of my arrival,

how we translated the hours,
haiku by haiku,

until a satisfying silence
hovered before dawn.

Those days afterwards
we sat hours

before moss and brushed gravel
to resurrect that deep silence.

But today I hear
birdsong, water splashing,

and my thoughts,
too loud to ignore.

Before me
a crowd of children gathers,

eyes squeezed shut
in laughter.

They stand in a circle
and clap with a rhythm

that hums daily
in the garden.

Weight

Even after the new money became official currency,
the old women continued to count it in their heads,
translating decimals back into shillings and pence.
They missed the clink of heavy coins in their pockets
like amulets against illness and despair.

When Vatican Two demoted Saint Christopher
and disposed of the melodious Latin mass
as gas lamps had once dismissed my grandmother's ghosts,
the old women shrugged resignedly and retreated
to the back of the church to mutter their prayers.

They relished the slip of beads through their fingers
as their lips moved through decades of the Rosary.
The holywell water at Tubbernewglass
was a great cure for headaches, so they said,
and it was good enough for us in oul' god's time.

Even I, so impatient with their superstitious claptrap,
replaced the old religion with devotional poetry.
I memorized my own magical formulas, grateful in the end
for a tether that allowed a little grazing room,
for any weight that would anchor me to the past.

Fire Song

On Saturdays the coalman in blackface
upended his sack in a dusty heap by our back door.
Father shoveled the jagged lumps into our shed
where jackdaws rose beaked and furious,
to squawk at him from the flapping dark.

Mother, acolyte to the gods of the hearth,
knelt down to rake the ashes after breakfast.
She carried cinders in a bucket to the yard,
twisted newspapers, criss-crossed kindling,
erecting an altar of coal and turf
that pulsed with a tabernacle light.

When father arrived at six o'clock we froze in place,
looking for clues to gauge his mood.
He stood with his back to the fire
rubbing his hands together,
rainwater pouring off his bicycle cape.
"The poor we have always with us,"
he muttered as steam rose from his trouser legs.
"and to him that hath not, even that which
he thinketh he hath shall be taken away."

She shooed the cat from his chair,
eyeing us into obedience,
then raked the fire to give us
alphabets on our legs
and make our chilblains burn.

She fed him with the meat that men must have.
We gathered around the table to watch him
mix Coleman's mustard in a wooden bowl,
the spoon trembling in his workman's hands.

Three thousand miles and a lifetime away
the radiators hiss and spit like vipers,
reminding me to mourn that hub of heat
around which we clustered, drawn together
by a light we thought perpetual.

Boredom

My parents might have been farmers,
they talked so constantly about the weather.
"What kind of weather is that fella giving us now?"
my mother would ask, as though
the dreary television weatherman
had invented the rain or painted
the color of the murky Irish sea.
How could I complain of boredom
when they worked so hard for just that luxury?

The cyst on mother's knee was like an extra nipple
emerging erect from the roundness of her kneecap.
For years before it was surgically removed,
I watched her wince as she dropped to her knees
for every bellrung summons of the Sunday mass,
troubling deaf Heaven for my immortal soul
while the seconds crawled the clockface
and I fidgeted incessantly on the seat.

When I woke up screaming in the night
she'd insist an upset stomach caused all nightmares.
Why couldn't she admit that life was terrifying
and suffering couldn't be sidestepped forever?
But she never listened, liking
the familiar throb in her own voice too well.
"Say a decade of the Rosary," she advised,
"and you'll be asleep in no time."

I think of all those cheerful letters sent
when I was paralyzed inside,

the land of opportunity laid out
before me like a body on a slab.
I've learned that inner weather is what counts.
Constant greyness is the consequence
when you're afraid of heat and cold,
and scenery is nothing to write home about.

Marriage

I could never figure out why mother
wore lipstick to bed, or why they giggled
in the next room when she read him recipes
from Maura Laverty's country cookbook.
"Your father has a nose for perfume," she'd say,
dabbing the little bottle behind her ears.
"He wouldn't give you thanks for a rose that has no scent."

If he was in the driver's seat,
she was the hub of the household wheel.
"I have my ways of getting around him," she'd tell us
when he fumed that all the dogs in the neighborhood
conspired to shatter his hard-earned rest.

She kept the pills for her nerves on the kitchen shelf,
and last thing at night she stood in our doorway
brandishing a bottle of holy water
to bless us against the night.

Of course it wasn't perfect,
and it wouldn't be true to say
as he often did after she died
that they never had a cross word in forty years.
"He treats me like a child," she'd mutter
dashing tears from her eyes with the back of her hand
as she beat the soda bread.

So I wondered one night when they woke us up
to feed us sticky toffee that had refused to harden,
had I dreamed them there at the foot of the bed,

laughing as they twirled toffee into sugar-canes,
their faces softened in the night-light?

And when I asked him what would I be when I grew up,
he lowered the pages of The Evening Press
and looked at me over his glasses—
"If you're half as good as your mother," he said,
"you'll be doing all right."

Ask No Questions

When we were kids we loved to strut about
in mother's high heeled shoes and necklaces,
dresses falling in folds around our skinny chests,
red lipstick smeared on our sugared mouths.

"Walls have ears," grownups would murmur
when you ran in from the street unannounced
and caught them whispering, their permed heads
held close together over the teacups.

"Ask no questions and you'll be told no lies,"
they told us when a neighbor who was "expecting"
disappeared in the ear-splitting ambulance,
and we stood about with our mouths open
imagining her helplessly propagating catastrophe.

When I asked for tampons, mother said inscrutably
that they were only for married women
and I wondered for years how the white dress
and nuptial mass could magically change anatomy.

"That one knows more than her prayers,"
they said of Mary O'Connor, the girl next door
when she implied that marriage held mysteries so brutish
you'd never drag them from her saintly lips.

"Ignorance is bliss," they clucked when we asked
if French kissing was a mortal or a venial sin.
Small wonder I arrived in the delivery room
like so many other girls, not knowing how I got there
or how in God's name to get out again.

Being Gone

When we were kids they said if God forgot you
for an instant you'd go out just like a light.

So when I'm due to be gone for a while,
say a week or two, I look around
for someone to be there waiting
just for me when I return.

It's not the everyday aloneness I mind.
I relish the hours spent wielding my razor-point,
notebook at the ready, eavesdropping
on other people's conversations.

It's more the need for a reference point,
someone to hold me in his mind's eye,
to ward off absence that comes screaming
around corners like an ambulance.

I never used to worry when I boarded a plane
knowing Mother was out there somewhere,
hovering near the wingtip, my tireless mendicant.
I'd press my nose to the plexiglas window

imagining her buoyed by sheer devotion.
But she's farther away now, preoccupied
with who knows what celestial housekeeping.
So I mutter aspirations just in case

some amnesiac might be listening,
his ear cocked to Heaven's floorboards,
hoping to overhear news
of a half-remembered humanness.

Still Listening

Gradually sound retreats as wax builds up
like silt in the narrow ear canal.
The radio dims to a dull rumble.
You tune out the lilt of your mother's litany:
tea-sugar-butter-flour-potatoes-onions-milk.
The sound of her speech rises and falls
like a wave washing a distant shore.

She likes to raise her voice in public
and glance around, head bobbing, to snag
chance interest in a stranger's eye,
trap him like a mouse
under the cat's paw of her tongue.
She's impervious, playing to the crowd.
You tug at her sleeve,
a bluebottle buzzing and battering
your wings against the glass.

You'll never miss your mother 'til she's gone,
old women hiss, wagging fingers in your face,
shaming you for something you haven't done yet—
but will.
For years you hardly speak
afraid you'll end up like her,
unable to stop talking once you loosen
the floodgates of lips and larynx.

But after escaping to America,
you hide in the Women's Room
crouched on the edge of the toilet,

head down, hands over your ears,
trying to shut out the high notes
of New York and Boston accents,
recalling her lyrical shopping lists
or the way she'd perch at the breakfast table,
head on one side, balancing her teacup,
a mother bird regurgitating last night's novel,
the worm she'd saved to satisfy your morning appetite.

Body Language

My father used to lift me up with his huge hands
to examine the blue eggs in a bird's nest
or let me pet the horses pulling carts in our neighborhood.
I'd rub my cheek against his chin's hard stubble,
inhaling the smell of Old Spice aftershave,
Sweet Afton cigarettes and hair-oil on his collar.
I thought his knowledge called the world to life.

But when I hooked mother into
the long-line cross-your-heart bra and corset,
she'd cup her hands under her breasts
and admire herself in the mirror.
"Give you a bit of a shape," she'd say,
and I'd turn away mortified at her lack of shame.
The aunts and uncles said I was skinny as a picked herring.

Easy then to pretend I was a boy with my brother's
Lone Ranger rifle cocked between my knees.
My father cut my hair just like his own,
running the metal clippers up the back of my neck,
creating as poor an excuse for a girl
as small boys for the cowboys
they impersonated on our street.

Now most days I'm fairly comfortable in my skin,
having come to terms with my odd angles.
It's like house-sitting for a close friend
in a place I'll occupy for a season or two.

Already I love the house that is your body,
an enjambment of bones and muscle, lines and linkages,
the hearth of your heart, blazing in your chest.
Even as mine mourns each lost limb it touched
or failed to touch. Especially its own self-hatred.
That, more than anything.

NORA MITCHELL

Offerings

You've been feasting on words again.
Mine, I hope,
a silly hope since these syllables aren't mine.
Birds are always headed for home,
flying north or south,
though I've assumed
their home was here.

You come out of the study,
stuffed with consonants and vowels,
similes and verbs,
repeating a beautiful nonsense line.
The small rain down can rain.

The birds amass with the impulse
home driving them.
In the harvested fields
they fill the compact houses of themselves
and then decamp.
Mellifluous, gaudy, sweet.

Near the Ipswich River in January
the winter birds grow so tame and hungry
that you can stand with arms outstretched,
palms spread with seed,
and the birds will alight,
tiny metallic feet
scribbling ideographs across your skin.
Swift strokes,
sparrow, chickadee, finch.

This Flat Earth

I bear my body toward you,
beaded mercury

gliding with the tilt of this flat ground.
Your skin rushes up to meet mine.

A siege somewhere far away, and its small victims
are airlifted in. Each ambulance

approaches our neighborhood with a low cry,
then passes up the hill.

Propelled now
in a slower motion, in the loose gravity of wanting.

The borders of your skin shimmer,
your muscles relax.

At the hospital entrance, under sodium lights,
the ambulances deliver their tiny damaged passengers,

and the drivers turn back to the airfield for more.
Across their backs

lines of weariness and sweat.
I wish I could touch the comforts

of flesh, the folds, rivulets, waves, and lips.
I wish I would go too far,

or far enough. I wish I had the right
biological currency to spend,

I wish I could sweep you
into the wet night and into the deep

volatile tangle of trees,
but as a lover I am growing inept.

The small victims are losing limbs;
we read about it in the papers.

Fireflies

Together, we watch them drift across
the new sheet of night—like periods, or commas
in the odds and ends of inaudible sentences.
My eye follows one, loses it,

then picks it out again.
Behind the small, slow-moving lights
layers of dark oak and pine rise,
and behind them the mountain's shoulder.

A week ago, on the summit
of Mount Abraham I watched a glider
wheel, quiet and sudden, over my head;
and as it floated off

it seemed to become as clear as glass.
A white flash in the sun, and then nothing
but blue. Can you picture the pilot
soaring without need of metal struts

or fiberglass? Just human skin,
solo, to press against the burning sky.
They say fireflies cast the perfect light,
illumination without heat.

Yet fireflies move through this night in cadenced
dialogue; dark, light, dark, and dark.
More dark than light, more light than heat, it's sex
and desire just the same. I am speaking,

through silence, to you now. Yes, I'm sorry
for that pilot, blinking off and on all alone.

Insomnia

Predawn, a window slides open
at the back of my throat
a breeze gusts through.

Cough, it says.

Resistance is useless.
My comrade in slumber
rolls over.
                    For hours, I've been undoing
the rhythm of her breath, but now
she sleeps.

Her desires, or my desires?

Predawn, the curtains sway inward.
The wind in my throat
feels like those spacious first weeks
after I stopped drinking:
cough, and the ache only gets
a better grip.

Arrowing flesh, out of my grasp.
Grasp, out of my arrowing flesh.

You
have slipped out of the house in the night
down to the bar
to have a beer I cannot have.
You are dreaming with another woman.

My scalded tongue, your salt skin,
and cactus flowers at the windowsill.
Miniscule jeweled bodies,

                       bright pink
humming of wings, they drink deeply
from something still dark.

After Rain

All over town the sidewalks
are slick with maple wings.
As I walk home from the hospital, my bones sing;
at times, I find my changed body beautiful—
the way the organs continue to swell
in the doctor's dim radiographs.
Beneath the trees, my whole body grows,
until my massive arms are dappled green.

My neighbor comes out of doors,
her newly washed sheets billowing around her
as she pins them to the line.
The babysitter's face bobs in a window,
and my two girls tumble tiny from the door
to run toward me. I scoop them up
and twirl them, green-winged, from my arms.
Wild with delight, they spin away.

Why Horses Sleep Standing Up

Our lungs can no longer bear
the weight of our bodies,

so we have taken to sleeping
on our feet, at odd hours, and like horses

we shuffle out of consciousness
into another enclosure, another pasture.

Of inextinguishable grass. Fierce
rippling. The *hiss* and *pith* of a pliant hide

seething with dream as it hits
ordinary air—thermal shock,

this coming back.
The riders are waiting, apples in their hands.

Appaloosa, roan, and chestnut cloud
the east. Gleaming pewter hooves.

Wrestling with the Angel

*—from Portrait of an Artist (Pool with
Two Figures), 1971, by David Hockney*

A beautiful young man streaks beneath
the surface of a pool

and another man peers in,
unnoticed, wanting him.

When the swimmer breaks the plane of the water,
slicking his hair back comfortably

with both hands, the other man has disappeared.
The swimmer rests

his forearms on the pool's blue edge
and stares across grass to a slatted fence

and the whirring street, counting
and counting his dead friends, until the chill

crawls from the cement, down his arms,
criss-crosses his back, and holds him again.

Before he can pry himself loose from the wall,
before he can trust himself in the graying air,

he begins to shake.
He wills all his belongings, the house,

the tables and chairs, to lift out of his sight,
but everything stays put. The earth is calm

and voracious, and he hates it.
It holds the lost, cherishes, grinds them.

After I Quit Drinking

It's a bird I swallowed,
one wingtip brushing the back of my throat.
When I was nine, I spent one whole night
staring at a photograph of my mother
and trying to cry. To help me sleep
my father arranged the Big Dipper, Pole Star,
Moon, glow-in-the-dark stars
around the ceiling light,

but I imagined her drifting past
the handles of both Dippers and right through
the Hunter's chest. I wasn't sure
that she was dead.
After I quit drinking,
my life fell apart gracefully.
It was due.
To fall is a form of wanting:
I wanted more air and more time.
I wanted to be a blue parachute of myself,
so that I would never have to come to rest.

I went down those stairs
looking straight ahead.
When I reached the bottom step,
I put all my weight
where I thought the floor should be
and had six more inches still to go.
Seven, eight years later,
I don't know if I crave
a drink or not.

After a friend of mine died,
I dreamed I was leaning back in her arms
and when I woke up, the truth was
she was still gone, I just didn't want
to miss her anymore.

Everything and Nothing

—after Anna Akhmatova's "Voronezh," for Joseph Fine

A reporter on last night's news
launched a bucketful of boiling water
into the air, where it hung,
froze.

This morning,
I walk warily over glassy ground.
Trees and powerlines are furred with ice,
cars stick in their parking places,
and above the TV antennas
of this northern town are ravens,
and cottonwoods, and a high blue
window that opens on everything and nothing
And all around us
sitcoms and daytime dramas unfold
in the brittle air, and we pass through them
the way we might
move through a graveyard, murmuring
excuse me to the stones
we stumble on.

In the room of the young man
returned last month to his childhood home to die,
love and revulsion take turns
at the hearts of those who stand and wait,
as the branches of the cottonwoods,
in blessing,
lift and meet above our heads.

DOUGLAS K. CURRIER

Ghazal for Daffodils

And there, in her place, she had put some daffodils.
I wandered for days, wishing sometimes to become daffodils.

My life became a guitar, my fingers became
her chords, wanted only to strum daffodils.

My mouth devoid of words, my lips
of no use except to hum daffodils.

And I was a minor god of nature, sure that wherever
I put my hands, up would come daffodils.

This spring, they came, but the yellow sunlight
would not speak, emerged mum daffodils.

And I counted what I'd lost—a single color, the sun,
the air, and a crowd of dumb daffodils.

I killed them all, cut off the yellow, nodding heads,
slit the green throats of the glum daffodils.

And so, Currier sits in the damp grass, surrounded by dandelions
gone to seed, and the heads of numb daffodils.

Gacela de la Tristreza

He has studied the ways not to mind tristeza.
Turn a corner, all he needs to find tristeza.

The streets of Buenos Aires or a town in New England,
daylight is the color of strip-mined tristeza.

She made a business of counting, of cataloging,
listing the knots with which she could bind tristeza.

But at his table, he would summon-up, enlist, welcome
pain, make a friend of much maligned tristeza.

The polished wood, where daylight faded, darkness
gleamed softly, and his wife and he dined tristeza.

Any hardwood, polished by years of shuffling, is good
for the muscles, bones of the back—straight-spined tristeza.

But he was sure, given any type of cloth—a bed sheet,
a lady's scarf—that he could unwind tristeza.

She would lie naked, flat, hands stretched above
her head, and beckon softly—reclined tristeza.

His eyes, open, dark, he knew carried
the pictures, the marks of an unkind tristeza.

This beckoning, be it in Buenos Aires or a town in New England,
was seen and understood by a blind tristeza.

And Currier, seated at his table in the morning, moved the playing pieces of daylight and aligned tristeza.

Swan

She received a love letter in school.
My daughter told me this, read it to me,
described how she had read it to her friends,
to the boy's friends, to her teacher, to the boy's aunt.
The boy is awkward and ugly—not popular
in sixth grade—and deserves to be humbled
and embarrassed.

My daughter is talented. She is intelligent and
already a great beauty, born a swan in such a way that
no one has ever questioned her species. Grown
men are unabashed in her praises, even to me.

But I am confused. I am the boy that she has hurt
into silence this night. I lie on my bed and don't want supper.
My aunt will tell my parents. This beautiful girl,
who won't let me dream, has hurt me into
a hardness, a denial, thin laughter with which to cover
my naked self. "It was a joke. I didn't really mean it.
All of you thought I was serious."

Are the beautiful always cruel? Are the talented
always indifferent to limits they know nothing of? I wouldn't
wish her less beautiful, less talented, but how can I
grab her by the shoulders and say, "I am that boy. I am
fat and ugly and too studious and dull-witted. Don't
read it aloud. Keep it. Throw it away. I know
what I am. I know how little I can expect."

Perhaps she will learn kindness. Perhaps compassion is not hereditary. I am lucky to be her father, for how else could the person I am, be anything in her life?

Walking Song

Too tired to be still for long,
my father's steps begin to weave,
his body walks the same old song.

And to these legs, these feet belong
and so forth—up till we believe
too tired to be still for long.

And in his hands—a grip still young,
takes, twists, holds on to some reprieve
his body walks the same old song.

As if to ask if it were wrong,
he stops, slightly, as if to grieve
too tired to be still for long.

He moves among the whirling throng
—a fighter, worker, loads to heave,
his body walks the same old song.

He remembers still when he was strong,
as strong as sons who start to leave,
too old now to be still for long,
his body walks this tired song.

Maud

Maybe she is my Maud Gonne, one
of those who drives men to easy women,
drink, religion; long, quiet poems
and poems that rage darkly. Men,
like I am, we know how to suffer, have it
as science. We know how to lose,
an acquired taste we educate our palates
to savor. We know we must be hurt
into emotion and welcome that level of hurt,
that when all is finally over, requires
the stoical smile we keep in our
back pockets for just such occasions.

Not that any affair is ever, really over for us.
We store them away—each image, each word,
each sensation crowding around consciousness
like guests at a buffet, like crows around
road kill, like maggots in a feverish
dance on any aging meat.

Our aging flesh teeming with regrets, those things
we're driven to—monkey glands, depravity,
vice in its many colors, belief in witchcraft—forgetting
is easier than what we must do to remember.

Metaphysics of Wool

Animal and dense, a muscular
fabric—wool remembers the shape
of a body, the smell of a body,
the needs a body has—to be
remembered, to continue sensually
in the world.

When you feel wool on the skin—
the wool feels back, luxuriates
in the warmth, takes smell
so softly, so deeply it lingers.
Wool's purpose—wool's gift.

The sweater you pulled on
after making love in the first chill
of morning. It sits now in a dresser,
trunk, or box doing its work
of remembrance—the alchemy
love works on the body, the chemistry
of longing to be resolved months
later in a drawer.

The blanket you left her in,
carries her scent even on a shelf
in the closet, imperceptibly
arousing the other clothes, hanging
so seemingly limp. Cotton knows
nothing of love, knows only that
bodies wash out of its plant life.
The body, human existence,

is beneath silk—the royalty of fabric
still struggling with lowly origins.
Man makes fabrics without memory
—rayon, nylon, dacron, polyester, all
with one idea—to forget.

The intimacy of wool. Give her
your coat to wear for an afternoon,
snow delicately decorating her hair,
the wool of the coat taking her
in, breathing her, to share with you
for weeks after she has gone.

Hard Season

This grace, the same clumsy balance
which allows walking the ice of morning,
crusted snow denies the unstepped.

Each hard day slips into the next, I slide
into myself — more deeply, sometimes stumble,
sometimes fall, until each hour is a domino — tall,
unsteady, thin base of the present.

The grace it takes to walk, the grace
consumed, the cordwood of warming,
of listing the cold; the time spent with weather,
the blue blanket of death, I am overrun.

You are weather. Savage and cold in this hard season,
condition I have lost the reading of.
Winter squall, not the coats of caterpillars, not
the thickness of moss on trees, not clouds,
not the colors of the sky prepare me for you.

Confused by layers of warmth, the depth
of sweaters, what fires to hold my poor hands in,
I lack this simple grace. Weather blind, I read
the signs and make no sense of shifts in temperature.
Ice was never really water. Snow never
really melts. Thaw is just another senseless word for love.

Aran Stone

You place each day upon a day, each stone upon another
convince yourself that this is life, is work,
pile dream upon hard dream, and the bottommost smother.

It's clear each stone has its weight, each day its own tether.
Clear there's nothing to tell you just which random quirk
of fate places day upon day, each stone upon another.

Clear each stone has its shape, each day its own weather.
A mystery how each takes form in the murk
of dream upon dream, the bottommost to smother.

Each stone has its earth, the days fit together,
watch the edges of stone, where lost meanings lurk
in the cracks of each day, each stone upon another.

Each stone fits your hands, the days become leather
that must soften at night, must be cured by the dark
that strangles dream upon dream and bottommost smothers.

Through each wish to die, each curse of your mother,
escapes you might try, just this you must mark —
you place day upon day, each stone upon another,
pile dream upon dream, and the bottommost smothers.

Afternoons

A task for the old, to recuperate afternoons,
to add memory to these, now late, afternoons.

Our naps a convenience to others,
as children, we learned to hate afternoons.

Then school, and some work finished,
indecisive, we began to debate afternoons.

And each, only a time of day, an accident
of weather, hard to locate afternoons.

Later, in sun-darked rooms discovering
how easily the ways of flesh infiltrate afternoons,

we slept siesta, decided that mornings with air
and bustle were sent to mitigate afternoons.

And later still, when siestas died on the tongue
and slept on without us, as if to compensate afternoons

for a loss of bodies skillful at the use
of time, able not to reiterate afternoons,

we found occupation after the midday — buildings,
streets, air-conditioning, as if to placate afternoons.

Did we know that this moment, this infinity,
would cease, the night begin to amputate afternoons?

Like lost limbs, we feel the tingling of sense,
the presence of drugs designed to alleviate afternoons.

And Currier there, a stack of old calendars, sorts through
his life, looks for constancy, seeks to obliterate afternoons.

Tango

for Noé

We spent our last thirty bucks
on an afternoon of tango lessons
in White River Junction. Two hours
with ten other sweaty couples in a room
that seemed somehow smaller
than our kitchen, we shuffled like bumper-cars
— unable to foresee the next three steps
of our life together.

And we have come to tango too late, I fear —
each of us loomed larger and older in the too many
mirrors of that dance floor. Besides,
we were learning steps to fit the way we already
live. Tango — that ritualized slamming together
of bodies and then pulling violently away — we've
danced it without music in the dingy kitchens
of a dozen small apartments.

But for you, I'd have felt stupid and baggy, my feet
large and soft. But I closed my eyes and you became the girl
of the letters in broken English, the girl who gave me
South America a street at a time, the girl who loved me
to distraction. And I became younger
and deserving.

We were, you know, the only couple that belonged there.
We had spent 18 years beating that sad, wise music
into each others' heads. We knew the steps in our necks
and spines, in our hands. Sweaty, close, mirrors,
people in the way, we have lived these most of our lives.

Tango smells of Buenos Aires and I remember the last time
we walked Florida, the American Embassy, el viaje largo
en colectivo, el Banco de Boston, the Dali exhibit, the
clinic, the blood tests, the American Embassy. I have always
loved you. I have always pulled violently away.

Late In The Day

Late in the day, the day dies late,
trees gather their leaves, pull
the green lawns up against the night
over roots to ease the cold wind
that gropes the surface dark with icy hand
and brushes gently an ease of naked skin.

And who of us finds comfort in his skin
knowing that what we shelter is lurking late.
A beast we cannot touch nor hold in hand,
watches the time — the push and pull.
There are sounds we cannot hear over wind
of day, now hidden by the creeping night.

Bring him to the surface, close at night
and we do this, but to touch each other's skin,
and leave him hang in a drying wind.
We might think to keep the monster in, that late-
comer, afraid of light, afraid the day will pull.
If you'll but give me yours, your hand,

that — you encompass in your hand.
Me into sleep and you the deep of night,
he waits long to yank and pull
all skin except our sheltered skin.
To save more is, I fear, for us too late.
The rest we leave to the darkest wind-

sounds, flying unknown to us in the wind.
Hold on tightly, opposite poles, by only a hand,

completely in this whirl of confusion. Late,
there are many sounds, those night
keeps from shedding, each of us, his skin.
Night, lone night, night of gravitational pull,

and wind, treacherous winds, that pull
— taking the best we have as toy. Wind
clutching at us, who drown in aged skin
without soul, without youth, but a thousand hands,
blossoms and leaves ripped from us at night,
loosened, fear for lives lived too late.

We find that death will pull, hand-over-hand,
disguise this age of wind and use the night,
wither this skin, that would lie gently too late.

Midnight Disease

When I am with you I write
my name in water, happy
with your eyes, hair,
happy to be within reach
of your voice, any word
I can hear, any sound.

My name is not important.
I can write it over and over
in water, trace it on any expanse
of skin you lend me, taste it
on your flesh, read it on your lips.

I can scribble it over and over
on paper, the blue lines—veins
under my fingertips.

Any name written on skin—warm,
womanskin—means to disappear,
wants to be fluid, rewrite itself in ways
that might briefly entertain, might
please, might pique any icy
interest in that cruelest of mammals.

A name is no match for a woman.
A man is no more than a name, a
brief sensation—not unpleasant, one
much like another, traced over and over.

SUE D. BURTON

What's Possible

First I wash as far down as possible.
Then I wash as far up as possible.
Then I wash possible.
            — My Great-grandma Beck

Anything, said the king
to Mrs. Simpson, shedding his crown
and she her chemise,
Anything for
you, dear, though that's
not who I thought of first when I
heard Marcovicci
*chanteuse*ing from her nether plexus
at the Empire Room.

Any? As in *every?* The whole world an
oh, my goodness?
Well, the room was awash.
She *only*
wears black when she sings, you know.
I like you
in black. Your cowboy neckerchief,
say. Only.

To sing like that! Those slow
rosy *O*'s. Swirls of apricot silk.
O, desire. Under elms. Under
anything at all, dear.
As far down as, if

you please. And sugar in
the tea.
O, The World. Ripe.

American Tragedy
after the painting by Philip Evergood

Awe — awe is the only word
that covers it.
I admit it, O.K.? I do have leanings toward
the overblown, but believe me,
I want to bow, want to fall to my knees,
fling open my arms, gape
whale-mouthed —
some dramatic Shakespearean gesture, sprung
from a place I didn't know was in me.

Only one other time, coming upon the gleaming
Aphrodite (the museum
in semi-darkness, the officious
guard refusing to turn on the lights)
have I felt such a thing.

Magnificent Girl/Woman! — I wanted to throw
myself at her feet — the City of Love herself,
her headdress a sculpted tower, an acropolis,
her hair the cult geometry of
an ocean (marble rivulets still glazed
with bright Archaic green),
Aphrodite of the Sapphic "plain style,"
frontal, direct. Pitiless as the sea.
Colloquial as the million doves
still roosting in her city's ruins.

There I was in Anatolia with a bunch of
American Sufis shrugging me off as a nutcase but who,

themselves, the week before at Ephesus had wept —
ten or fifteen of them kneeling and bawling, trying to
remember the rosary
at the most mundane (I'm sorry,
I'm a horrible snob) rendering of the Virgin Mary —
a stock Mary,
not even as inspired as the plastic
moon-goddess keychains hawked outside our hotel —
just like a zillion other anorexic Marys on a zillion
other downy clouds, just one more weepy
go-between, pretending to be one of us —

I told you I'm not a generous soul.

But whatever it was that could move tourists
who had given up on their Catholic pasts — who'd even
given up on their
Jewish pasts and were crying, too —
that part was very odd —
whatever it was — *Hail Mary, Full of*
Grace — a mostly middle-aged group — surely not
as simple as longing for their own mothers —
I understood when I saw the Aphrodite.

But what about *American Tragedy?*
Well, here I am watching a slide show of
protest paintings at a military college in rural
Vermont, the discussion is: If the Rosenbergs were
guilty — Jesus! — would you
still say this is art? (How about,
If they hadn't been Jews, would they still
have been fried?)

And now — why haven't I heard of him before? —
(whale mouth!)
Philip Evergood! It's my goddamn home
town! (pardon the expression, it's really
Chicago) (but the same strike, 1937, the Memorial Day
Massacre, the same blustering blues and badges and
billy clubs)
It's me! It's me. It's all my
unfinished poems.

A tiny mill at the top, like a child's
tinker toy fort, like the view of Republic — endless
tombstone-sized gray roofs — from the "poor
section" of the Erie Street Cemetery,
only this fort is
manned by the larger-than-life, twisted,
sneering
        (The La Follette Senate Investigating
        Committee Report: "The Republic Steel
        Corporation has a uniformed police
        force equipped not only with revolvers,
        rifles, and shotguns, but with more
        tear and sickening gas than any
        law-enforcement body in the country.")
            Republic's President Tom Girdler: "Sure we
got guns."

Tommy Gun Girdler's "plain style."

Front center: a man's white straw hat, fallen
to the red-soaked macadam, the man — white shirt, sleeves
rolled (balmy holiday afternoon) —
shielding his pregnant wife, the Madonna in grass green

with white high heels — who ever wore
high heels to a picket line?

Evergood's own "plain style" — simple, direct.
Unpolished — he wanted his work to
reveal struggle. Unnatural use of color (the
primaries) to "create mood" — "clashing" reds, harsh
dominant blues. "The hat in the
foreground," Evergood said, "magnifies the violence...
and I always liked the painting of the woman...making her
pregnant, I thought, would accentuate the horror."

Of *whose* claim — of *what* — is she the icon now? —
the pregnant woman lying on the ground
under the upraised billy club,
under the upraised blue arm already
slamming down,

under the steel eye,
center canvas, her spring dress.

Millet

I.

on closer look, dried wings

white worms and sticky cocoons,
long strands of millet cocci

I dig out dead bugs with a spoon,
pick out hard brown bodies, clumps of gummy pearls,
rinse the gallon jar in scalding water, sick
as dried wings rise to the surface.

I wash some down the kitchen sink, then
imagining they'll miraculously resuscitate, crawl
up the drain into jars of rice and corn,
I flush the rest down the toilet —
what if the plumbing gets backed up, a glutinous
mass of millet in the pipes?

Pressure-cooking cups of picked-over millet,
I tell myself, even if worm eggs
are still in there, they'll be boiled to death, they
can't hatch inside me, saying at the same time
— steam splattering the wall —
why don't you throw it away?

A feeling like dread I can't swallow down.

II.

Old eggs, born all at once forty years ago,
millions aging all at once, unacknowledged children
only psychics see, contracepted, aborted, buzzing
around my head, in the spirit plane, like gnats

or sitting in my belly,
round white pellets longing for their
chance of a lifetime, that moment of grace
when they, too, get to burst through casing,
when they, too, will shout out, *mittelschmerz,*
mittelschmerz, as they make their way
down the tube,
calling a magic name, with an elemental sound
like Rumpelstiltskin.

In their jubilation, they hear only a melodic
made-up mantra like
fallopian or *praise the lord,*
and they forget in their preconscious memory that
mittelschmerz means pain and, in an empty tube,
is a code word for doom,
the same end that came to a lonely dwarf
who asked for the first born and got nothing
but a rage that tore him open, starting
at the crotch.

III.

I adapt to the luteal moon, brew cups of tea
in the dark, and wrapped in my old flannel robe, pace
by the kitchen window.

Yet sometimes at three a.m., I wake overwhelmed
with the terror that riveted me to the middle of my bed
as a ten-year-old, imagining,
lurking at the sides, the plump prepubescent fingers
of Bobby Walker and Pete Mahaffey
still waiting to creep up from underneath
where they've been crouching now for thirty years,
short-legged angry men,

or if not that image exactly anymore, the same paralyzing
fright that holds me in the center of the mattress,
hearing my own
voice in the shadows demanding my first born,
which is still only myself.

In the morning, I mark the calendar,
count the days, waiting
for the brown wings, waiting for the dried
brown wings, fragile, almost transparent.

Eurydice

His look *upon* her (one more demand) and then
overwhelming her, though
even *before* — even before the story
says — there's exhaustion.
For though
the path is level, has been trampled even,
she's been scaling a precipice (legs leaden,
led) —
leaning forward, grabbing
clumps of grass to pull herself along,

clutching at squat bushes with orange berries manic
with reflections,

things-to-do still inked on the backs of her hands:
buy toilet paper, pick up cider at
the co-op, fix
dinner, fix his loneliness (fix,
fix)

oh
the relief — the overwheming
relief of it — she *can't*
go on —

    then *Farewell-l-l*
slick as afterbirth (does she sing now
even more
beguilingly than he?) her
well   well   well insistent

as a bad dream —
(but the story is *his*,
his, his)

it's all
in the timing —

and the cloud passing over her eyes —

I've Finished My Birthday Cake,
and Now I'm Reading Frank O'Hara

Really my green-apple-and-red-hots (Jan baked it! He did!)
all-nostalgia Ohio *pie*.
        April 13, 1994, and I think of you
because I'm 51 and red-hots happy.
           And because I am reading
Frank O'Hara's poem to his friends who are getting married, and
you are my friends and cannot get married, and are having your
tenth anniversary this year.
        And because it's my birthday
and you have moved away, and I miss you.
           Because I want you here
eating cinnamon pie.

        And because this is Samuel Beckett's
        birthday, too, and he and I have the
        same initials, and he died and I never
        sent him "Sam's Last Krapp" that I wrote
        28 years ago, and maybe he would've
        written back, but now it's too late. And
        because 28 years ago Frank O'Hara was
        still alive, and I didn't even know who
        Frank O'Hara was.

I love you, Frank O'Hara, come back!

And because, Weeza, you and I have lived many present-lives
together, because you un*caw* my critical crow,
because when you met Alice you warned her, women's group
hears all! (oh! our earring-trinketed, sequined Weeza

and her Alice who shops at Lands' End — but soon ah! oh!
our Alice's courtingerotica from the north. Those slow rosy
O's! Swirls of apricot silk!),

and because of our good years at the Women's Health Center —
how many women's hands have you and I held during their abortion?
how many women have remarked on my grandmother's garnet
ring? —

and because you are a doctor now, and I'm a P.A., and our
poems are too vast to fit on Rx pads.

But Alice's poems we eat.

And because, Alice, your heart is bigger than one of those
blue-tiled walk-in Guadalajaran ovens. Because your heart
is bigger than a MOMA Earth-tone William Morris revival kitchen,
because your heart *is* a kitchen, full of comfy chairs
and pear pistachio torte
and we clamber inside to be fed.
Cooking is to you as "Personism" is to Frank O'Hara —
a poem at last between two persons, not two pages.

And because you're the realstuff Managerial Woman, the Dean
& DeLuca of ways-to-get-grants, the Marion Zimmer Bradley
Queen of Sci Fi — to say nothing of your black mushroom
pierogi and your sun-dried tomato comfit and your
garlic-roasted cornish hens and your ... and your ...

Ah me, now I'm having another wee sliver of pie, a little
smackerel of something, as Pooh might say.

Because you wore your favorite February sky crewneck
to my 50s tea and a flaming-amaryllis ostrich feather cloche!

(The look on Weeza's face — Alice in red tailfeathers!)

And because you both love Jan and me together and baked
goddess breads for our wedding and laughed and cried with us at
our Our Lady of the Peppers altar and always think of us
as family.

And because we all love to eat!
O our dinners!
Weeza declaring, "If food were a woman, I wouldn't
stand a chance."

Dinners at your place, rosebud Spode and The Dead Can Dance,
Alice's watercress sauce and Kronos Quartet, Weeza's fresh
blueberry pie, blasé noninvasive cats NEVER CORRUPTED BY
LEFTOVERS! lounging on their carpeted cat perch by the
window, dreaming of dry Friskies.

Dinners here, Jan's famous Chicago-style latkes, the famous
Chicago-style corn oil latke fire, my anything-with-basil (tho
you were spared the ice cream I made one time for Bill), our
chile pepper chopstick holders, our cosmic chilies blinking
year round.

Cherry Garcia with hot fudge at Ben & Jerry's, chocolate-dream
cake at Pauline's Cafe, chocolate-dream cake at the D.P.

Dinner the night of the cloudburst that moon-muggy July
when you and Liza and Jan and I threw off our clothes and ran out
into the streaming yard — Jan's malefantasyoftheagescometrue,
naked with Sue's women's group!
                              O luminous
quotidian!

And Meow! Mewow! to ze moon!

O your cuties manylife'd! 18 lb Channy my fav. Sweet tabby
with Frank O'Hara now.

Frank O'Hara, come back! Don't die young!

O our friendship manylife'd!
Weeza's endless stories of the hospital. Weeza's endless
hours at the hospital.   Weez endlez hospit.   Wee
hophpit zz   zzz   zzza.

And the Christmas turkey so trimmingsed the Frigidare wouldn't
close.
        Alice grinning like a cat.

Now Jan and I are clinking four glasses of champagne.
With both hands raised and arms homesick wide we toast you —
Alice and Weeza, our lettuces by the water, our
raisincakes and quinces, our sisters, our
brides,
we're dancing the hora and the Ahiah drop-kick in your honor.
We love you! Don't die young!

ABOUT THE POETS

Sue D. Burton is a Physician's Assistant working in women's health care. Her poetry has appeared in *Calyx, West Branch, Kalliope,* and *Sojourner.* An interview she conducted with poet James McMichael is scheduled for publication in *Agni.* She holds an MFA from Vermont College.

Douglas K. Currier lives in Burlington, Vermont, where he writes poetry in English and Spanish, and organizes poetry readings and workshops around the state. His MFA is from the University of Pittsburgh.

Nora Mitchell is author of *Your Skin is a Country* (AliceJames, 1988) and *Proofreading the Histories* (AliceJames, 1996). Her poems have also appeared in *Calyx, Dark Horse, Hawaii Review, Hurricane Alice, Nantucket Review, Ploughshares, RFD,* and *Sojourner,* among other journals. She directs and teaches in the MFA Writing Program at Goddard College.

Irish expatriate **Angela Patten** was born and raised in Dublin. Her poems have appeared recently in *Prairie Schooner, Voices International, The Eleventh Muse,* the *Wexford Review* (Ireland), and others, and came second in the 1996 Patrick Kavanagh Society Poetry Award (Ireland) competition. She holds an MFA from Vermont College.

Kenneth Schexnayder has published poetry in numerous literary magazines, among them *The American Poetry Review, Black Warrior Review, Nimrod,* and *Southern Poetry Review.* He has taught at the University of Montana, University of Memphis, and Old Dominion University. He is editor of *Vermont Quarterly* at the University of Vermont.

Emily Skoler works as a high school tutor and guidance counselor, and is a poetry editor for *Sojourner.* Her poems and essays have appeared in *Cimarron, The New England Review, Passages North,* and *Third Coast.* She has an MFA from Vermont College.

Editor **Daniel Lusk** is a poet and teacher. He directs the Summer Writing Program at the University of Vermont, where he administers Evening University and Academic Programs of the Division of Continuing Education.